GW00870268

There's More

There's More

A Little Something Called Grace

Sergeline Michel

XULON PRESS

Xulon Press
2301 Lucien Way #415
Maitland, FL 32751
407.339.4217
www.xulonpress.com

Paperback ISBN-13: 978-1-66286-166-6
Hard Cover ISBN-13: 978-1-66286-167-3
Ebook ISBN-13: 978-1-66286-168-0

DEDICATION

In memory of my loving friend and confidant Louisa Prince, I am content with knowing that you are again with your maker, your impact on my life and love for me will live on in my heart and mind forever.

TABLE OF CONTENTS

ACKNOWLEDGEMENT

The process of writing and completing this book was a scary one but it is also the most rewarding thing I have ever done. None of this would have been possible without the support of my darling adopted sister Daisy Rodney who stood by me during every struggle and all of my successes. From the moment I decided to turn my journals into a book, she has been a mentor and editor, helping every step of the way to make this a reality.

I am eternally grateful to my adopted parents, Randy and Junie Rodney, who took in an extra mouth to feed when they didn't have to. They taught me everything that I know and raised me to be the woman I am today. I am so happy that I will never know where I'd be if they did not take a chance on me and gave me a roof over my head and became the parents I desperately needed at that age.

To my mother, Rose Carmene Fanfan, I am so happy to have reunited with you and continue to get to know you better. Thank you for providing the financial support during this process and for supporting me in every single one of my ventures, and to the rest of my biological family, my dad, and younger brothers.

To my best friend Michelle Jean Jacques, my close circle of friends, and special mention to Jayanie Sharplis and Nashida Bertrand who continue to encourage me and push me to be my best self, I am grateful. Thank you for being my true friends! And to my mentor Kerry- Ann White-Lewis, thank you for speaking life into me always and for being one of the first to have read and critiqued this book.

To my extended family, my sisters, Jeanette Raffoul, Rena Baptiste and Sherniah Charles, My brother Caleb Rodney and brothers in law Albert Raffoul and Sherlon Williams, cousins, Amy Shillingford and Michelle Jno. Baptiste and church family at TGFG; You all played a huge part in my upbringing, and continue to be the best support system and family I need.

While this period of my life was filled with so many challenges, I can now say that it was all worth it. Writing a book about my life so far has been an extremely hard process, but with the help of the team who worked with me at Xulon Press, I was able to face every hurdle head on and make it through. Thank you for believing in my story and helping me bring it to the world.

To everyone else who has played a role in my life, listing you all would take pages, but thank you for being in my life and part of my story.

Poetry/ Spoken Word
Collection Titles

Part 1

- Why me?

- Grace Blessed this mess

- Voicemail

- Beyond these scars

- The best man

- If Life had a voice

- These tears

- Where are you?

- Purpose

- Suicide Note

FOREWORD

Pastor Rose Carmene Fanfan

As a mother, one of the greatest things to witness is seeing your child do well and succeed in all he or she does, but as a Christian parent and Pastor, for me it is also seeing my children following Christ willingly and giving themselves to God and ministry. God is a wonder-working God, and Sergeline is my miracle child. Her birth continues to be one of my biggest testimonies. God delivered the both of us during childbirth and took care of everything like only He can.

Life has many challenges and as a parent, sometimes there are tough decisions that need to be made. Leaving my children behind in search of a safe place and good opportunity was one of those moments for me. My children were young and explaining the situation to them at the time was not easy or something that they could fully understand. But, in everything, God shows up and does what He does best, and that is take care of His own. My children reunited with me, and in the end, we had to separate again, but I am still trusting God to have my family reunited.

You're holding in your hand a life-changing book. With every turning page, not only did I learn something new about my daughter, but reading this book also made me see what I thought I knew through her eyes, and how she felt about everything that went on. Even from my own experience, sometimes what I thought was another day in the land of the living, I now see was the first step on a journey that would bring me to where I am today.

As you read this book, I hope it reaches your heart! I applaud my daughter for being brave, for taking this step in sharing her story and God-given talent, but above all, for allowing God to use her as a tool to not only bring Him glory through her writing, but in the process, evangelize and let others know about Him and what He is able to do. I am thankful to the many people God has placed in her life when I wasn't near; they too have played a tremendous role in her story and have helped shape her into who she is today. I most definitely believe in the saying, "it takes a village to raise a child!"

My prayer is that after reading this book, you find some sort of encouragement, especially if you are facing some difficulties. I encourage you to read with an open mind and open heart, and I pray that, like me, you learn and receive something.

PART 1

I Was Lost, But Now

Life never goes as planned, and sometimes the things we hope for take time; sometimes they come unexpectedly or even faster than we imagined. There is this famous saying that "time waits for no man," and it's funny how a simple clock on the wall makes everything seem either too short or too long. Well, my mother's dream was to have a child after she got married - a child of her own - but it took some time before I made my grand entrance into this world, and for her, when it did happen, I was the answer to her prayers.

My mum always reminded me of Jeremiah 1:5 which says, *"Before I formed you in the womb, I knew you, before you were born, I set you apart; I appointed you as a prophet to the nations."* She believes that this is the foundation of my journey thus far, one that began with its challenges from birth. Every year for my birthday, my mum reminds me of her difficult labor and pregnancy. She informs me how she was found lying on the floor, almost nine months pregnant, in a pool of blood. She had to be rushed to a hospital where she was unresponsive, and I had to be delivered in time. Her favorite part in the story is how thankful and happy she is that God saw her through, and we both made it out alive. The most interesting part in all this to me is when she also reminds me of the promise she made to God, as a way of thanking Him for saving her life. She promised Him that she would dedicate me to the church. She would not pierce my ears, mark my skin, or allow me to do any form of body modifications. Sounds like a modern-day Hannah and Samuel story, doesn't it? (1 Samuel 1:2 – 2:21) Every year, for my birthday, she would fast and pray and then have the biggest celebration for me. No matter where she went, my birth continues to be one of her biggest testimonies.

However, my journey to *me* began when I was only eight years old. The journey to something new! I didn't quite understand what it was or what it would be, but I remembered my dad coming home one day, and saying that we were moving to another country. At first, I remembered being excited because I was going to finally be united with my mother who had been living in a different country for the past three years. I remembered the sadness that came over me after realizing that, not only was I leaving my dad behind, but I was also leaving everything I knew and was a part of -- my classmates, cousins, grandparents, and friends. I missed my mum, but I couldn't understand why we had to leave everyone else behind. My mother left for Dominica when I was six years old; I had an aunt who was already living there and when she found out about some of the issues back home, she invited my mother over to the island.

With preparations already made, I traveled the next day with my two younger brothers, with a complete adult stranger who had to accompany us to where we were going. I was excited to be on the plane -- excited for the thrill of it, and excited to see my mother, the woman whose face I could barely remember. The plane ride was quiet; although it was my first time on a plane, I wasn't nervous. I was more concerned about what would happen when we landed. I had questions. Would she look like what I've pictured based on the photos? Would she be happy to see us or treat us well? When we finally arrived, I remember being lost at the airport, looking for what seemed like a familiar face. My brothers were crying, and I was trying to stay strong. The man who accompanied us was looking and searching, and I also started crying, until I felt a warmth from a hug so tight that I knew I was safe, and that she had arrived. When I looked up, my mother picked up the youngest of my two brothers and held my right hand, while my left held my other brother's hand. I remembered it being night and the view was amazing: lights everywhere, which were things I wasn't used to back home in Haiti. I didn't understand then that this would be my home from now on, and that would be my view, and these would be the lights that I could see every night.

Don't get me wrong, Haiti is a beautiful place. It was lucky for us that we lived in what is considered the rich part of the city, Port-au-Prince. The thing about electricity in Haiti, from what I can remember, is that the government has control. At a certain time during the day, the government would give lights to the place, and it would be during that time that you'd hear people saying, "Yo bay kouran!". If I can remember correctly, Port-au-Prince obtains less than twenty hours of electricity per day, and only about thirty to forty percent of Haitians have access to electricity. Blackouts back home would occur frequently, and those who could afford it, either had generators or solar panels, so I think that's why I was so enraptured by all these lights being on in the streets.

Everything felt so new and so good. I was happy, taking in every single moment. When we got home, I carefully analyzed my mum's face. I asked her questions about her life there, where she worked and what she did, and we stayed up talking the whole night. Thankfully, when I woke up the next day, it was not a dream. I was indeed in a different place, somewhere far away from home, with a language I could not understand and people who did not look familiar. I knew then that I was *lost*. Lost in my thoughts and everywhere else. The conundrum was that I did not like our life here, from day one. I questioned my mother about her decision because life back home was much simpler. We had a maid and a house, but here, my mum did everything. She had a beautiful life back home, an amazing job, and respect from the people in our community, but here, I was looking at our new life here and it was hard to accept. Now, you may be wondering why someone who had all that would leave their country? Well, the persecution and crime rates back home were becoming ridiculously high, and no matter how financially stable we were, my mother always thought that security and safety came first, and hence, the quest for a better life or opportunity began. I tried my best to understand that aspect of the change, but eight-year-old me had a hard time adjusting.

We came during a summer, so there was not much to do. I tried to get used to everything: the neighborhood, my mother's daily routine, the church we went to, the people in it, and the school that my siblings and I would soon attend. It was hard! When September finally came, and we went to school, it was not what I expected it to be. I could not understand anything from the teachers' or my classmates' mouths, but what I understood was their actions. The saying is indeed true, actions speak louder than words, and has no language barrier! The way they watched me, laughed, and stayed away, the way they pointed fingers at my hair because of the hairstyles my mother would give me, hid my belongings, and sometimes dumped my food, was the only thing I understood. I was silent; all I could do was cry and say nothing. I'd speak in French, and no one helped or seemed to understand me. The only place I felt safe and happy was home. I'd share my experiences and that of my brothers with my mother, but there wasn't much she could do. She would go to the school to talk to the principal and the teachers, but they also could only do so much.

Time passed, and I began to learn and pick up on a few things. Before I knew it, I could speak up clearly. The first English words and phrases that I knew and understood were those that were commonly uttered; they were the "F" word, *"go back to your country,"* and *"that ugly Haitian girl."* I felt like I did not belong, felt worthless, and I wanted to go home. I reached a point where I no longer wanted to be Haitian anymore. I hated my nationality! When people asked me where I was from, it became much easier to claim my Dominican Republic heritage and background from my mother's side of the family. I cried every night in my mother's arms, begging her to send me home, send me to where I knew I'd be somewhat safe, and I remembered her saying, "*improviser, adapter et surmonte*r," which meant "*improvise, adapt, and overcome!*" It's a phrase I've grown to love in its Latin origin. She would often add "Pran kouraj, gen pasyans!" which meant "Have courage, be patient!"

To me, these were not simply four words; they were the ladder that I needed to reach the shelf of peace. I had to remind myself every day that I needed to adapt, the whining and the crying, according to my mother, only made me look weak, and Haitian women are not weak people. I knew then that I needed to put on the strength she was trying to pass on, and these three words remained with me. It wasn't easy; I remember a Dominican boy went as far as bursting my brother's head with a stone, and they'd also chase us after school. We lived in Checkhall, Massacre, and attended the Massacre primary school. We walked home most times because it was only a few minutes away, but it got so bad that we would wait for everyone to leave or look for a shortcut instead. There is this saying that "with time, comes change," but we waited for the time that change would come, and it felt like it was never coming, so we endured, and endured some more. Slowly but surely, it did. I began to adapt, and I made my first ever friend: a girl named Leila. She saw beyond my nationality, tried to speak to me in patois, which is similar to Haitian Creole, and brought me around her friends. I began to do well, and I thought then that I overcame it.

But, it wasn't until I thought everything was going well that it began to get worse! My dad came to meet us from Haiti, and one year later, my mother decided to leave again. Her reasoning was now that my dad was there, she could continue her journey in search of a better life. Part of me understood, but with her leaving I had to now take care of my two younger brothers, and I also had to learn to live with my dad all over again. With my dad being there, all the anger that I felt about living in Dominica resurfaced. I saw his life downgraded before my eyes. *How did a powerful and influential journalist become a carpenter?* I thought. A man with degrees and education is now working menial jobs. I hated it all over again. To make matters worse, I began a hate-love relationship with my mother after she left. When she called, I did not want to speak to her or wanted anything from her. I became rebellious at just twelve years old! I was young, but I wanted to prove then that I didn't care about her anymore, that I didn't need her, that her counsel before she left was no longer valid, and that she was no longer my mother.

I placed my father in a difficult situation. I wasn't performing well at school that year, and I was about to sit the common entrance exams, which is the state exam, before entering high school. My dad, with the job that he had, sent me to after-school classes so I could get better, and I was not budging. Lo and behold, I did the worst possible thing I could've done. I created the biggest lie a twelve-year-old child could, and that was claiming death about a family member.

I've heard people say that no sin is greater than the other and that there is no such thing as a simple white lie.

Well, I don't know how to phrase this, but my lie came with consequences, and I faced the consequences throughout my last primary school days. I felt like the year my mother left was a strain on me; I started having trouble finding what I considered as inner peace, and I didn't know why everything was falling apart.

I would cry and cry repeatedly, without having a reason for those tears. I missed my mother so much that sometimes I'd just shut down, place myself in a corner, and sometimes stay quiet for days.

I realized something was wrong with me when I broke the trust of everyone who cared for me with that lie. I was in after-school classes with Mrs. P for my common entrance exams at school, and I was sitting outside crying and screaming. One of the students went to call her; she came and asked me why I was crying. I didn't have a reason; I didn't know what to say, then I remembered my mouth going on and on, and I was giving a story without thinking anything through.

That story was believable! My teacher believed and cried with me; she called my uncle, who picked me up; I went home and said nothing to my father. It wasn't until the term was over, when my dad went for my report card, that my teacher told him everything. He wondered what she was speaking about, confused and in shock. He listened to the story that I made up and had no clue where it came from. My dad told me that his heart "dropped and leaped out" of his chest at that moment, and told my teacher that what I said was all fabricated by me.

When my dad came home, he told me what had happened and how disappointed he was that I would do such a thing; it killed me more inside. My conscience and I were at war, and I did not want to attend school the next term because I feared what was awaiting me. I had no choice but to go to school, and it was the worst day I could have ever had. I could see the teacher's eyes on me, talking about it all day, and eventually, I was brought to the principal's office for evaluation, which became a norm for me. I started attending counseling and being placed under observation.

I couldn't blame it on the fact that I was only twelve years old, with no mother figure present or whatsoever. I really couldn't pinpoint any reason behind this *lie*. Eventually, I started to wonder how people would ever believe anything I said? How would they trust me again? I told myself that I was going to spend the rest of my life paying for it, that people were going to assume that every time I spoke, it would be a fib.

I thank God it did not end up that way. I am thankful for my teachers and principal; they saw something in me that was bigger than that lie. They helped me through that phase, and day-by-day, I made progress. I stopped crying in school, having tantrums, and I have never, up to this day, created a lie that big. It became a thing of the past. The saddest part in all of this is that the person I said who died passed away a few weeks after that incident, and my dad blamed me, and said I called it.

I can't lie now and say that I have never *lied* since, because that would be a *lie*, but off and on, I've lied to my father about simple stuff teenagers do, which we now joke about, but it was never anything of the magnitude where I had to make up a story. I knew that I dealt with, and was still dealing with, a lot of bullying, hurting myself, suicidal thoughts, and struggling with self-love. My dad often reminded me that he understood how hard it was, how difficult it was to come to terms with everything that was going on at home, but part of me never really felt like he understood. I found myself going back to the four words and remembering my mother's advice; I knew then that it was time I was open and honest with her about how I felt.

My mum realized the effects that her leaving had on me, so she made it her duty to rebuild our mother and daughter relationship. Don't get me wrong; although my mother was not present in body, she did all what was required of her and more, sending money, sending groceries, and whatever was needed. Although these things mattered, I simply wanted to feel close to her. So, she sent devotions in the morning, messaged throughout the day, asked about school, my crushes, and the little things that made me feel like she was around; eventually, things started to get better.

At the back of my mind, I knew some people would judge me, and others would continue to hold that one thing against me, but I never forgot my teacher's words: "Your mistakes don't define you now, nor will they define who you *will* become. once you have accepted your wrongs and decided to change."

The lie was one thing; it was a pivotal point in my life, and although I was rebuilding my relationship with my mother, I was still unsure of myself, and I continued to wrestle with things. With everything that happened, what I was unaware of was that Mrs. P, my sixth-grade teacher, knew my pastor and had gone to him, explained the situation I was in, and things took a different turn.

The thing about God is that He finds you in your mess, even when you don't want to accept it. I was born in the church, and my parents -- especially my mother -- were very much involved in church, and still are, to the point where she is now ordained as a pastor. I knew God and I understood what was required of me, that one day I would be baptized and maybe get involved in ministry. But, when my mother left, my father changed religions, and we started studying with the Jehovah's Witnesses. Their teachings captivated me, and I was interested, but at the same time, I started spending weekends at my pastor's house and attending church with them. I reached a point where I was questioning the whole idea of God. The conflict that went on within me when it came to having faith and what to believe in was overwhelming, but then things went from zero to a hundred in my parents' marriage that same year, and everything I worked so hard to change about me was bursting back out like an old flame.

I got depressed; I was now in my first year of high school and I knew I couldn't go back to how I was. I became the intercessor and communicator between my parents, and the back and forth was not healthy. It got so bad, to the point where I needed to feel pain, that I needed something to physically match what I was feeling inside. I had to decide if it was getting a tattoo or self-harm, and I did both, but it didn't make any difference because the pain was still there. That pain left me numb. I remember feeling my father's wrath that day, but I couldn't cry. I couldn't bring myself to show *any* emotion. I knew then that I was bound to turn out for the worst. What made matters worse was that my first-ever crush hurt my feelings, and told me that I was going to spoil him with voodoo if he ever ended up liking a Haitian, and that to me was a big blow. I strongly disliked boys from that point! I realized that the stigma with being a Haitian was still following me! No one tried to get to know me for me, but instead associated me with voodoo because I was a Haitian. I hated where that was going and the emotions it was bringing out of me.

Lucky for me, it all changed after my pastor and his family took me in permanently. I don't think they knew the extent of what I was facing, but some way, somehow, they knew I needed help. The dark hole that I was in started to receive light, a light that was trying to pull me out of what at the time seemed like a comfort zone. It wasn't easy, I needed a lot of molding, guidance, and love. At first, I failed to see all that they were offering and providing for me. I was so used to that pain that anything that looked different was not so welcoming. I didn't speak much; my face was always unpleasant. I'd shut down and push away. I didn't like the image of unity they created while knowing my family was not only broken, but separated. I didn't want to be loved because I didn't think I was worthy of it, and so I got myself into trouble at school again.

It was weird how it always took me getting into trouble to realize what I needed to change. I was part of a group chat with some members of the youth group in church, and there was a conflict amongst us, and I took my anger out on one of the members by cursing him out with the very first English word I learned, the "F" word. I didn't have a phone then, but I had WhatsApp on my tablet, which was supposed to be only for school purposes. I took that tablet to school the next day, and one of my friends at the time had it reading the messages from the group chat. It was during break and a teacher was passing by. I stood behind her to look at what she was doing on the tablet because the use of electronics was only permitted on campus for school purposes only. The teacher saw that she was on WhatsApp, took the tablet, read the messages, and took it to the principal's office. That was the first time my name was called on the microphone, and sadly, it was not for anything good. I was taken to the principal's office where my guardians were called, and they came. The principal showed them the messages and they conversed for a while. I could see the disappointment written all over their faces, and with one look, I knew I was about to be punished. Here I was again, in trouble, but this time for cursing and being angry over a matter that did not concern me, but I think that's what happens when you put yourself in other people's business. My guardians were disappointed and took away my tablet. I was asked to apologize to the guy, and the church youth group chat was disbanded. The young people were somewhat upset with me, and I was conflicted. I realized that I couldn't continue down that path, but I didn't know how to go about getting the help that I needed to change, and that's when Grace found me.

What I realize about us, young people, is that we don't like asking for help, and some of us don't ask for help because of the bad experiences we've had when we've asked for it. Life to me then seemed like a circle. It was a cycle of the same thing repeatedly: a cycle that went from bad to good, to worst to good, and then to bad again. One of my guardian's older daughters, whom I consider a sister, became my rock, and according to her brother, he called it, "on the counter with Daisy" and that became a thing. I'd ask questions; we'd argue things out and she guided me, corrected me when I was wrong, and showed me what I needed to do. It wasn't only her, but because I started to open myself up to receive counsel and guidance, and I started to accept the love that I was being given; I saw the community that was trying to help me grow. I started seeing my guardians in a positive light instead of the enemy, and that's when I decided to accept Jesus Christ into my life as my Lord and personal Savior. That summer, I got baptized, and I joined the dance and ushering ministry in the church. At first, getting baptized was only so that I could be involved in ministry but after a while, I started to see a difference in myself. There weren't any major changes, but I started to think positively and developed a new perspective towards life. I didn't just see my pastor and his family as my guardians anymore; they became family, my adopted family!

As time went by, I began to see the hands of God in my life, and in the relationships that I had with my family and friends. I became excited about my faith, and I thanked God for calling me out at such a young age, and making me new. My mother was excited; she felt like the promise that she made to God was on its way to being fulfilled, but that happiness didn't last long, because I ended up piercing my ears on Christmas of 2014. We debated about it over and over until I decided that it was about time, I knew what the Bible said about these things for myself, and how I should live. Personal Bible study became a thing for me; at first, it was just to be able to prove my mother wrong on her beliefs, but the deeper I got, the more I wanted to know.

I remember a preacher speaking about gifts from God, and how everyone has a gift that they should use for the honor and glory of God. That message got me thinking. I didn›t know what my gift was or what God was calling me out to do, but I knew there was something. I always liked reading and I read in the dark all the time, with my flashlight under my sheets, which I believe is one of the reasons that led to me wearing glasses. I became extremely close with a sister at the church, whom I loved calling "Aunty Octavia." Not only were we born on the same day of October 17th, but she had a passion for children that I just loved. Her daughter, Sherelle, is a major book fan like me, and when Aunty Octavia found out about my love for reading, she would hand me some of the books that Sherelle had when she was younger, and I couldn't have been happier. I kept reading and reading, and one day, I came across a quote from Maya Angelou's book "Letter to my daughter," which stated, "You may not control all the events that happen to you, but you can decide not to be reduced by them." [1]I was so touched by that quote. I felt like this lady knew me, and at that point I needed to know who she was. I Googled her, and I fell in love with her writings and her life. It wasn't only that; it sparked an interest and love for literature and writing. In my second year of high school, my literature teacher at the time, Ms. Natasha Nation, made literature fun, and the way she taught, explained, and found different ways to bring stories to life captivated me. So, I believe if there was a class I enjoyed in school, it was that literature class. Not only did I want to be like, or *be,* the next Maya Angelou, I wanted to write something, but I didn't know how to.

I prayed to God, and I remembered asking Him to birth something in me. "Give me something to say, something to write, just something," I said. Not getting an immediate response, I lost the zeal and the fire that I had within me to write. I continued reading some more, but this time, it was not with the passion that I once had. Trouble came again, but this time I didn't cause it. The bullying that I thought stopped in primary school began again during my mid-high school years. I knew I had my sister to rely on, and I had a few friends now who would stand up for me, but I was hurt, and I felt empty. I thought not only was God not answering me, but He was also allowing the bullying to happen all over again, even though He knew how it made me feel. When I realized there were certain things about me that the students were bullying me for, I tried my utmost best to fit in because I couldn't bear being different and being picked on again.

Then I fell upon my favorite book of all time, *Be Real Because Fake is Exhausting,* by Rick Bezet. The book opened my eyes to a new reality. I realized I was trying to wrap myself in a blanket that didn't suit me! I was becoming someone else during school hours because of the bullying. I tried to put up a front at school, acted differently, and joined the crowd that I felt at that time was the right one for me. I started to create petty white lies, creating the ideal boyfriend and friends, just to be with them. Pastor Rick Bezet's words in *Be Real Because Fake is Exhausting* helped me realize the true meaning and importance of being my true self. I also realized what I meant to God. A line that has stuck with me from the book is, "We live in a world of fakers. Rather than being real with each other, we present a carefully crafted persona that hides our faults and magnifies our good qualities. But inside we long to be loved, warts and all." [2]I realized that I needed to place value on myself. I needed to live an authentic life through Christ, who freed me from the spiritual death that comes with pretending. I was so concerned with my feelings and how I felt, that I didn't take time to notice and think of how much I was hurting the one who loved me and knew me best, and that was God. There is something I have come to realize about us Christians, and that is, sometimes we do things, and after realizing that it is wrong, we ask God for forgiveness, but don't take into consideration that what we did hurt God. I had to remind myself that God is my father, and like I wouldn't want to hurt my earthly father's feelings, I would not want to do the same to the One who created me.

I felt like I was putting on a mask that needed to be taken off at the end of the day, and it was not healthy. Over time, I have realized that lies catch up with you, no matter how good you think you've created it; it always comes to light. What really happens in the dark always comes into light! God began to call me out on that fake persona and revealed not only my true self, but the truth to the people I was trying to be the "ideal" friend or person for. When God exposes you, He does it well, and so when my mask fell off, I could no longer pretend nor lie my way through acceptance. The journey to accepting my true self began. I needed something to channel everything I was feeling, something to help, and finally, I found it. What I was craving for a long time was the ability to write something. It was no longer merely wanting to write something, or to be like Maya Angelou; it became my therapy. That for me was a big change because before I'd run to self-harm or something like it. Not only did I start to understand God more then, but I also felt free. That's when I wrote my first-ever poem, entitled "Why Me!" Poetry became my peace and writing became my best friend ever since. God answered my prayer right when He knew I needed it, and I knew then that was my gift. I showed my sister my poems and she liked them! Although my grammar was not so strong because I struggled with English, when it came to writing my thoughts sometimes, I knew I was on the right track. She asked me one day if I'd like to perform one of my pieces in church. I was nervous and I wasn't sure if I could, but she promised to stand with me, seeing as it would be my first time performing something I wrote. Father's Day was around the corner, and so she asked me to write one on that topic. I took up the challenge and wrote my first ever spoken word "Daddy, Let's Talk!" With my sister's help, I delivered, and the applause and comments that I received afterwards were another sign from God that this was indeed my calling.

I started to use my gift to glorify God often. I performed for Mother's Day the next year and other events that were taking place at church. Other churches heard of my writing, and one asked me to perform at one of their youth events that our church was also invited to. I also got the opportunity to come on as a guest on a talk show, with a group called Salt Ministries, and it felt good. I felt like I had found it all, that I had found me, peace, my gift, family, and God. But, little did I know, that what seemed like the end was only the beginning.

What I mean is that sometimes, you may neglect the fact that there are unresolved issues that have not been dealt with; for me it was within my family. The distance between my parents was still an issue, and continued to put a strain on my younger siblings. When my mum left, I never thought it was a separation, but her moving away to better herself, and hopefully, one day we'd be a family again. I still believed that there was hope for our family, that a miracle would happen, and my parents would fight this distance thing together.

The relationship I loved to see was crumbling down and I was so busy looking for the best in it, that I did not see the problems that were right there in my face. What hurts more now is seeing them both happy individually. The fact that it was so easy for them to accept being and living how they were made me sad. I am not selfish, and I wanted them both to be happy, but at the same time, I wondered if they could be happy by trying harder with each other, or for each other. My mother sometimes made comments that added a lot of pressure when she would talk to me about not understanding her reasons behind the divorce, and I knew she wasn't trying to turn me against my dad, but the back and forth did not make it any better.

At the time, my goal was to support whatever decision they took as long as they were happy. My mum found love and started anew, while my dad was still unsure as to what his next move was, so it was rough, but I tried to maintain an open mind. Every time I think of my parents, I must remind myself of the Bible verse in Ephesians 6:1-3 that says, "*Children, obey your parents in the Lord: for this is right. Honor thy father and mother; which is the first commandment with promise;That it may be well with thee, and thou mayest live long on the earth.*"You're maybe thinking, *well this is a common verse, and everyone knows it*, but what this verse does for me is not only remind me that I must love them despite how I feel or what I want, but of the blessing that comes with it. So, whenever I thought of the bad things in the situation, I kept reminding myself of the blessing. As much as I wanted to get angry, sad, or mad, I tried to maintain a healthy and positive relationship with them both. I'd rather be blessed than be cursed!

My two younger brothers are opposites! One of them recently hit rock bottom and it has not been an easy road ever since. I've had to deal with people I never thought I needed to because my brother was always in trouble. My father was present in body, but he was of no help whatsoever most of the time, because my brother lost all the respect he had for my father, and only remembered he had a mother when he was in a financial struggle most times. I tried my best to be available emotionally and physically, but I felt helpless.

What caused me more pain was the fact that my brother himself called me out, and said that I didn't know what I was doing, and that I was trying to make myself look good whenever I tried to help. He reminded me that I was living a better life, that I didn't know what he was facing, and that I didn't understand why he had to do the things he did. That created a hole in my heart. I felt every word, and part of me believed that it was true. I looked at the life that I was living, and mine somewhat looked better, and I began to fight with myself. I felt bad; I began creating this idea in my head that I needed to be in the mess with him because that was my family. I reached a point where I didn't want to live with my adopted family anymore because of that. I felt like I needed to be with my brother, and maybe if I was with him, then things would be different. I tried everything possible so that they would let me go, but they didn't. According to my favorite author, what I needed to understand then was that, "God accepts us exactly where we are, but he loves us too much to leave us there." [3]So, I knew God would not leave me in doubt or let me go down a bad path, and during that time, I kept feeling like I needed a change. I needed a reset.

The funny thing about growth is that it takes time. I thought that because I now knew God and had found my gift, that I was good, and I wouldn't feel down or depressed. I thought these circumstances would no longer seem big or even matter. I felt like things would not bother me so easily because I had found my peace, but it was not so. I knew there would be a time I'd have to put my faith into action, and that I'd need now more than ever, a little bit of hope.

I'd seek counsel and everyone gave the same advice. They told me that I needed to understand now that what I saw as a mountain was only a flat for God, or that I needed to pray and leave it all to God, but no one said, "Here's what you could do to help your brother," or what I could do to even put myself at ease. Some even went so far as saying my brother's problem and parents' issues shouldn't be affecting me this badly, and that sent me into a frenzy.

I realized then that some adults have this notion that teenagers shouldn't have issues, or issues that caused them that much pain. The common questions would be, "Do you have any children to think about? Do you have any bills to pay?" But, is that all that matters?

When I separated the misconception that a young person had to be working and paying bills or the like to be affected, or feel hurt, was what made a world of difference. I realized that it was okay to be sad because of these events, that it was okay to want to help my brother as much as I could, but what was not okay, was not realizing that I was also young and that not every battle was meant to be fought alone. I remembered how much of a mess I was, and God turned my life around; and therefore, my brother's life was his way of channeling the pain he was going through. I realized that he was much younger than me when mum left and that he was searching for a bond elsewhere. My goal at the time was to be helpful, to find a way to put my family in a better place, but I never took the time to think of what I was doing to myself in the process, and I never even took my brothers' emotions and feelings into consideration. I never knew how they felt about the separation, with all three of us living in different places, not with our mother or father. I felt even worse for not thinking of that because I saw what these situations were doing to me, and yet, I never once asked my brothers if they were okay emotionally, or allowed them to express themselves to me. I would often ask myself, "What kind of big sister are you?" In the end, not only was I taking everybody's pain and making it my own, but I was also stuck in a place of no return, and that's when I realized that I had lost my gift.

I couldn't put pen to paper anymore. The words that I felt needed to be written or said were no longer in me. I began to question my faith, asking, "God, You said to trust in You, to have faith, so why are You doing this to me?" I began to develop a negative spirit toward everything, a spirit of gossip, and I started to lose my close friends. I found myself doing things that I never saw myself doing. I went back into the hole that I feared. I got quiet again, and started to push people away. I began to go to counseling again, but this time, that counselor broke my trust. Instead of hearing me out and helping, that counselor became a messenger and a microphone to echo my worst fears and pain to people that we both knew.

At the time, the best gift I gave myself was surrounding myself with mature and wise people. As much as I couldn't find a way to bring myself to talk about things, God in some way, somehow, brought people who not only could tell, but sensed that something was off with me. It was at this point that I found the answer I was searching for: that for me to truly find peace, I had to let go. During that time, I felt like I was really on the verge of letting go, and I was ready, but one day after school, while I was walking home in my uniform, I had an encounter like never before! Out of nowhere, a man whom I didn't know came up to me in hopes of pursuing something. He began to speak sexually and attempted to touch me inappropriately. I was scared, so I moved to the left, and he moved also. I moved to the right, and he also moved. The road to my community was not usually busy around that time, and inside, I screamed for a vehicle to pass. When I gained control of my emotions, I pushed him away and ran home, not stopping one bit. As soon as I opened the door, I told my adopted mother that I needed to rush to the shower, and explained to her what happened. I felt dirty! I was someone who always hid my body, and my older sister used to joke about that because I wouldn't let myself be seen easily. That experience did not only add more of an alertness, but I began to feel extremely uncomfortable in places with men I didn't know. If someone came near my body and we were not close, I shivered. That day brought back so many memories of things that happened to me in Haiti when I was seven, and the trauma I faced back then. It was like I was reliving it all again! Although my dad found the guy and confronted him, I never felt at peace, and whenever I'd see him, my heart would race. It is a fight that I am still trying to win every day, but I have come a long way.

One of my favorite descriptions of God is that He is a funny man, with a great sense of humor. He is funny because he finds what I consider the weirdest things to bring about a change of heart or behavior from me. The best thing I know about life so far is that when we start to see ourselves the way God sees us, it changes how we live, how we think, and how we operate (Gen. 1:27).

I often find myself thinking that if life had a voice, would things be the way they are or be somewhat different? I love the song "Amazing Grace," and I am sure by now you've realized that. I feel like that song embodies everything about God's amazing grace and love. The beauty in God's transforming grace can change something so unworthy of love into a perfect imperfection. When I understand completely that it is never in God's plan to see His children unhappy, hurt, and confused, etc., I then understand the purpose. My purpose, and what was meant in Jeremiah 29:11. I also realized that we were made to live in community with each other, and God alone is not all we need. Yes, having a relationship with God is important, but we can never doubt the importance of having people around in our circle. It is hard to find honest, real, and authentic people in this world, those who would ride the storms with us and help us in times of need. If there's one thing I know, it's that when we open up ourselves to God, He guides us and shows us the way.

I am making this reference because in everything I explained above, while God was my source of strength most of the time, He used people to help me see what He wanted from me. I have a mentor whom I love so much, siblings, parents, and a best friend who proved to me each day that life is not meant to be done alone. Sometimes, when we are going through something in life, we just need someone to listen, someone who maybe has gone through the same situation or needs a fresh and new perspective. Because God created us to have people in our lives, He helps us discern who is right for us. If there is one thing I've noticed, it is that God uses broken people to do His will and His work, and that is broken people like me! You are never too messed-up or too far gone for grace to work.

Poetry/Spoken Word Collection I

WHY ME?

I searched and searched for an inner beauty,
Everywhere I thought it could be,
But who am I truly?
A question that bothered me.

The good, the bad, it all came tumbling down.
My life, the one I felt like I no longer owned,
The pain, like a knife, was cutting right through me,
Bringing loneliness and an emptiness,
That is so overwhelming,
But there is only one question,
A question that bothered me.
Why me??

I trusted who I needed to trust.
I lived like I needed to:
Changed! Renewed!
Yet, I looked at my life and saw a mess.
I sought help; I prayed.
Yet, everything kept crashing, one at a time!

But, I persevered! I kept the faith,
Remembering there's a life out there for me.
Someone out there who sees the true Sergeline.
Reassuring myself that there is a promise that will be
fulfilled,
While counting on the Father that never failed me!

Though I doubted and doubted Him repeatedly,
He keeps reminding me of who sits on the throne,
That He stood amid my pain!
And though the answer to my question may not
seem clear,
I knew that I needed to live each day like it was
brand new!
Just like His mercies and grace come anew each day!

So, I made up my mind to make it!
Fighting and waiting for the answer,
Hoping and praying,
That everything falls back into place!

Where the question that bothers me
Would no longer be "why me?"

GRACE BLESSED THIS MESS

Who am I?
Am I just the girl from that poor country?
The fat one? The short, thick one?
The girl who can't speak English properly?
The smart, yet stupid, one?

Why Me?

Labels upon labels!
Names upon names!

They called me what they wanted.
They treated me as they please.
They said I simply don't fit.
A nobody trying to fit in.

I believed it all!
I doubted myself!

I didn't believe the good that was being said,
because I was so consumed by the bad.
The poison that was fed to me
manifested itself into something greater.
It became part of me as the symptoms crept in:
Low self-esteem, depression, isolation, and more.

I lost faith.
Reached the end and was ready to give in.
All I wanted was to change,
to be whole again,
Free from this mess.

I didn't want to question the purpose; I wanted to find it.
I didn't want to escape; I wanted to fight it!
So I begged and begged God to show me how,
To help me be who I needed to be.

And there came the voice,
The light that overpowered my darkness.

The hand that picked me up and dusted it all off,
Gave me a song,
Words to speak,
And a story to tell.
A little something called Grace, who blessed this mess!

THE BEST MAN

I've met guys who liked me for my brain.
I provided them with answers to solutions and I was
a thinker.
I've also met guys who hated me for my ethnicity,
the idea that I would hurt them with voodoo.
I've met guys who liked me for my mannerisms,
reserved, calm, straightforward, protective.
But, I've also met guys who hated me for my beliefs,
obedient and God-fearing.

Then came a guy who took those likes and dislikes
and turned them into something I can't describe.
He loved my brain because it provided clarity.
He loved my ethnicity because it is part of my story.
He loved my mannerisms because it is part of me.
And he loved my beliefs because the foundation
was in him!

I didn't have to look for him,
He found me where I was.
Out of the darkness, he pulled me up.
Out with the old, birthed out the new.
He turned my Lies into Lessons;

Why Me?

He made my mistakes, a steppingstone to greatness.

While I was busy searching for those things elsewhere,
rejecting him,
He kept on Loving me boldly,
holding my hands,
wiping off my tears,
healing my scars.

Step-by-step, he whispered.
Did I ask why?
Why me?
Why do you love me?
Why do you care for me?
Why do you stay when all I do is push you away?

His words were,
"You are mine!
Mine to love!
Mine to hold!
Mine to cherish!"

Never have I met a man who cared for me so deeply,
who was proud to call me his own, and still does boldly!

The man who gave it all up just for me,
The man who would do it again just to save me.
The one who forgives me repeatedly,
The one who erases my past and guides my future.

The Lord God, my Savior,

My protector,
My defender,
My shield,
My peace.

The Best Man.

VOICEMAIL

You've reached the voicemail of 1-800-DEATH!
Oh, my! That was close!
A pretty close call? You could say that.
So, I guess it wasn't my time? My time to go!

But hey, I've been ringing this line for a while without
even realizing,
What was I thinking?
Oh wait! I wasn't thinking.
I've been in my head fighting a war.
My will vs. His.
My thoughts vs. His.
Yet, every time I lose!

Ring, ring, ring, it goes.
Why do I keep questioning it though, instead of
fighting through?
When I should be looking for an escape, I'm here
looking for a scapegoat!
But, if you ask me, I'm stating the reverse.
I'd say it be death knocking at my door when I'm the one
that be slamming!

I'd cry out and play the victim when I'm the instigator
that be spamming!

You've reached the voicemail of 1-800-DEATH!
Well, I guess it isn't my time.
I'm sorry I've been ringing this line.
I thought this was the way out.
The way out to something that was not like what I'm
going through!

So, death if you are listening to this voicemail,
I've changed my mind and I apologize.
Because now I know the good Lord is on my side.
Please ignore me for a while, because it isn't my time!

I'm going to fight through.
I will search further than where my flesh wants to.
I'll ask for help and maybe then I'll pull through.
So, the next time we'll meet again, it won't be this hard.
You'll be available because I'm certain by then the
timing will be right!

You've reached the voicemail of 1-800-DEATH.
Please leave a message!

Beep!

BEYOND THE SCARS

I have one question, and one question only.
Do you see me?

Yes! You!
Do you see me?
Think about it carefully.
Do you really see me?

Don't try to complicate.
It is simple,
but you dictate
descriptions upon me that fit your imagination,
descriptions that suit your ego and expectations,
of what you wish for me to be.

I've tried to be brave,
doing my utmost best to communicate;
yet, you don't appreciate.
Appreciate the person I choose to be!
I'm not asking for love,
but acceptance;
yet, why do you continue to see me as a mistake,
a burden to you, and someone who's not worthy of love?

And now, it's too late.
I'm on the edge.
Lost and uncomfortable,
buried in shame!

Not only once, but twice,
you spoke these words: "YOU WILL NEVER BE
SOMEBODY."
These words continue to ring in my ears like I am
indeed a nobody.

Why Me?

A voice Amplified, disturbingly accepting.

But, do you take the time to think,
think of what these words could mean
to me, the child who once could dream?
Dream of being like you, or even better, in a blink.

I guess the thought never crossed your mind,
Or was it at this point you could express how you
truly feel?
I guess you can't see me,
see the one that you once loved and cared for.
The me that you'd go out of your way for,
but I see what they say about anger is true:
you speak your innermost thoughts and desires in
these times.
So, I am concluding with the thought that that's
how you feel.

Think about it carefully;
do you really see me?

IF LIFE HAD A VOICE

If life had a voice,
would it speak?
Would it say our names?
Would our existence have meaning or even purpose?
Would it continue to be selfish, biased, and cunning?

If life had a voice,

Would it call us out?
Out of our messes!
Band-aid our hurts!
Free us from bondage and the thoughts that keep our
minds captive!
Thoughts that block out silence,
Sorrows that prevent joy!

If life had a voice
would it warn us of misery?
Of deaths that sting!
Would the rich get richer and the poor poorer?
Would the broken remain broken or become whole?
Would it remind us of things forgotten?

If life had a voice
would politicians still be corrupt?
Where the system sets us up to fail!
Where judgment is done by us humans and not God!
Where the weak continue to be the prey!
Where color creates segregation,
and violence the new norm!

If life had a voice
would it sing of rebirth?
Where every son and daughter know their worth!
Would there be a song of freedom and justice?
Of unity and peace,
that no matter what comes and goes
Would living be meaningful?

If life had a voice
Would it resemble a sweet melody?
Where the songs that were left unsung
Ring bells in our hearts!
Would it reach out for hands unseen?
Reminding us of what's important!
Would it show us the way?
Save us from who we use to be
In moments no one sees!

If life had a voice
would it give us something new?
Strength for today,
Hope for tomorrow.
Would it give a covenant unbroken?
While the future is still unfolding!

If life had a voice
would it speak?

THESE TEARS

Choices? I have two.
To be or not to be?

How can I even be sure which one is right?
When every suitable explanation is unidentified?
In search of something that will make it clear,
something that makes it easier to bear,
the pains and hurt caused by something so dear.

Yet, all I have are these tears,
the tears that fall, whenever I think of the storms,
the moments once shared, but never cherished,
for the times passed with no memories made!

So, all I have are these tears,
That fall off my cheeks into the unknown
While it goes away off and on.
One thing remains:
the pain that causes these tears.

So, while I try to find new ways,
To keep holding on,
dear God, please don't let go of my hands,
While I am trying to climb,
secretly trying to find
something, somewhere,
help me get a little deeper
while I search for something greater.

One that is big enough to fill this hole
and to take away these tears.
I am open and willing to do what it takes.
Please hear my plea and set me free!

Cause all I have are these tears!

The tears that fall off my cheeks into the unknown,
but while it goes away, off and on
There is still one thing that remains:
An unexplainable reason for these tears.

Choices? I have two.
To be or not to be this sad or happy!

WHERE ARE YOU?

The stillness
The emptiness

Troubles left to right
Not a glimmer of hope in sight.
I searched and searched for a sign
For something that would satisfy.

It has become a silence that I can't tolerate
A reminder that something is missing
Something precious and rare
That keeps the heart yearning and yearning.

I'm at the end and I feel it near,
And this is what I fear.
To be confused and lost,
without knowing what it'll cost.

To be alive without the one,
The one who brings peace.
I know of you; I've heard it all.
But why do you seem so close yet so far after all?

I'm on my knees.
Pouring out my all, crying out my eyes.
Praying that you give a sign

Something to remind me that you exist

Just one sign.
Show me that I am not alone and that I'm in
In your arms where I belong
So, give me that sign, so that I can take that
one bold step
Out of the depths of despair.

I pray it's not just a scope of imagination
Thinking that you're somewhere within this nation.
Please just be that one companion
That helps me make that progression

From lost,
To found.

PURPOSE

It's a mission, one that's meant to be fulfilled,
Long before our birth, it has been established.
It's a mandate, written out and given by the highest
In its uniqueness free to all mankind.

Sometimes we lose sight of it
We wander around, searching aimlessly
We run from and question it
But it's a soul tie
With its way of finding us and binding us together
For what is already written cannot be undone.

No matter how hard we push
It continues to pull us
Right where we belong.
There are times that we feel delicate and incapable
So, we find ways to walk away
But this voice keeps calling
It gets louder and louder
reminding us that it›s who we are and what we were
created to do.

We then beg for the spirit of discernment
But deep down we know
We know it's his voice
But we can't stop gaslighting ourselves
Going based on our perception and judgment
When it's right there in front of us.

The one reason why we were created
Each their assignment but one mission
His one heart's desire is
To see us happy knowing who we are
And where we need to be.

So, He continues to strengthen us
Guiding us
Leading us towards our sole purpose
For what is destined to be will always be
For it's not our plans but His.

SUICIDE NOTE

Dear Bully,

I'm on the edge.
You can't tell, but I am close to the ledge!
I'm ready! Ready to give in and fall apart.
I know I've seemed fine, happy and all that.
You've always seen the highs, but never my lows.
But if only you knew how close I am to the end,
you'd probably talk to me, cry, probably beg.
Beg me to reconsider and remind me that I have
a "friend!"

Sadly, you're too late.
I've reached my limit.
I've thought about it.
Yet, still the pain won't go away unless I end it.
So, please don't hate me, it's my fate!

I know it's hard to say goodbye.
So, I won't stick around any longer.
I'm leaving this note behind.
Hoping by the time you see it, I'm no longer here.
It will sting, but I will pray you can bear,
but, also remember, you always preferred me dead
than alive.

It's ok to admit the truth,
maybe then you'll be set free,
from the guilt and shame of knowing me!

Why Me?

Don't think I've wasted my youth.
It was already gone before you and I even knew!

So, I leave on a good note,
on the premise that this is for the good!
While you were turning a blind eye,
mines were opening and I saw where I stood.

This is where I bid you farewell,
so here is my goodbye.
You're maybe wishing now you had more time.
Maybe to make it right or cause more harm.
But this is something I pray you'll never know,
wanting to live, but at the same time not
knowing how to!

Sincerely,
Your Victim

Part 2

I'M FOUND

The above poetry and spoken word collection was dark, wasn't it? Somewhat I believe! I went through a phase of this kind of writing because it was indeed my therapy, and my way of expressing how I truly felt. With every situation I explained above, there came poems and spoken words like the ones above. I had to learn to trust and let myself be free in God, and that brought an appreciation to life and an understanding that there was more. While scrolling on Facebook once, I came across a quote that someone I followed shared, but it continues to be my favorite and my motivation every day. It says, "Seeking greatness for ourselves may bring temporary acclaim, but serving God results in a lasting gain." While I may not know the author of this quote, it is evident that the person came to the same conclusion as me. That it is in serving God that we gain all there is. I've found peace by simply being his faithful servant and by trying to stay on the right path. Finding oneself is not easy, but it becomes easier when the King is the one guiding. I've heard people say that I haven't started to live life yet or experience anything big, so how can I speak of trials and God? I always respond the same way: no one has the same experiences; they may be similar, but never the same. Everyone has their story, and one that is unique to them. Faith cannot and shouldn't be forced on anyone, and age does not determine your relationship and growth in Christ. My favorite story in the Bible will always be the story of Joseph. (Genesis 37 – 50) I relate to his life's journey on so many levels, and he was a man who I want to emulate. Like Joseph, I faced many difficulties, and no matter what stage you are in life, circumstances and situations will always pop up. The difference between now and back then, for me, is how strong I have become in my faith, and how I deal with the situations and tests that life throws at me.

Another one of the faith-testing moments in my life so far was when I thought that I was ready to go to university. I've heard people say that every disappointment is a blessing in disguise, but to me, there was no way I could believe that there could be a blessing in the situation that I am about to explain. After seeing how well I did in high school, my mother decided that going to college in the United States would be a good option for me, especially since she was living up there. We decided to enroll in a few community colleges and universities in Florida and New York. To be honest, I wasn't sure if I'd get into any, so I still made plans to attend the Dominica State College, which is the local college where I lived. As a young Christian, I was taught to have faith and be patient, but for some reason, I decided not to get my hopes up.

A few weeks passed and I was asked to send my high school transcript to some of the schools, and so I did. Even with all that, I was still in doubt, and kept things on the low. Only my family, my mentor, and my best friend knew about the applications and the anxiety that came with them. They were my biggest cheerleaders; they prayed with me and for me.It was summer, so I started to occupy my mind with other things, and thought of ways to distract myself. My best friend came down from Barbados that summer without telling me because she wanted to surprise me for my graduation, and so we spent some time together. We were out that day, and I was with her at Krispy's (a fast-food place) when the notification came onto my phone. I didn't bother to look at it because deep inside I felt like it was going to be a major disappointment, and I wanted to enjoy myself. I kept moving like nothing was on my mind, and the more I did, the more my hands scratched me. However, when my mind is made up that it's going to do or not do something, that's what it is, and I made up my mind that I would not read the email until I got home.

I went home, took a shower, sat on my bed, and opened the email. For a dramatic person, I swear all the drama left me that day. I froze; tears were running down my cheeks, but I wasn't sure if I was happy or sad. I continued reading the email, then called my mum, and we spoke about some things. We decided to wait on the two other schools to decide.

I went from doubting myself to having so much faith in everything. I received an email from one of the other schools stating that I did not get in, but I held on to the little hope that I had, and I received an email from my other school of choice, stating that I got accepted. Out of all the three schools that I applied to, I got accepted to two, and they were both schools in the same state as my mother. One of the schools came with a partial scholarship option that I was going to apply for and so forth, but somehow, I decided to wait.

I called my best friend and before congratulating me, she started to make noise with me for doubting myself and not believing that I could've made it, and then she said what she always said to me: "I support you! I got you!" Trust me, she was there every step of the way.

Then it happened! Roadblocks after roadblocks! I cried and felt like things went from good to the worst possible. What made me angry was that it was not a financial burden because the opportunity for my school fees to be paid was right in front of me. My father made the mistake of not taking care of some important documents that I needed to complete a procedure that I needed to do before I left, and therefore, I got stuck. I couldn't go for my visa, and I had to write a letter to the school that I chose to decline my acceptance.

I was hurt by the fact that I was unable to go, and at the time, I couldn't see the "blessing in disguise" or the "reasons" behind it happening. I decided to go to Dominica State College where I strived to perform at my best to maintain a good G.P.A., and I did that. I was not sure what my life would be like if I did go to the United States in 2018, but I saw myself evolve in ways I didn't know possible. I got involved in activities and groups that I didn't think I was capable of. Jeremiah 29:11 says, *"For I know the plans I have for you,"* declares the Lord, *"plans to prosper you and not to harm you, plans to give you hope and a future."* I realized that I set plans that I wanted to accomplish without first seeking God. I told myself that I was ready, and believed that I was ready because of an acceptance letter. It took some time for me to realize that when my plans are not in line with what God has planned and what He has set for me, then it won't work. It took me a year or two years to make that realization and I wondered how God could not want me to further my studies or even be with my mother again, and He answered me. I was young, immature, and without experience. He taught me patience. He taught me how to make use of my waiting, and to always put Him first in my decisions. Knowing the type of person that I am, if this happened when I was still on shaky ground in my faith, I would have responded differently. When I finally accepted things for what they were, opportunities came knocking at my door. I got an internship at a news place and that gave me a start toward my career in journalism. I also gained a mentor in that field, Mr. Durand, who continues to motivate me and push me toward making my goals as a journalist and writer a reality. I started a blog, tutoring, and so many other things that have helped me grow and shape myself into who I am.

This journey continues to be one with many difficulties. I am still young, so I struggle with different temptations, impurity, negative thoughts, and anger, to name a few. However, I eventually realized that it was okay to not be okay, or to not have it all figured out. What is not okay is to feel like I needed to have all the answers at eighteen or twenty.

Another faith-testing moment was when I tried to become a citizen in the country that became my home away from home. I lived in the Commonwealth of

Dominica for thirteen years. I entered the country legally with a visa, and since I was a child, I was also on my parent's work permit. Haiti, although part of the CARICOM countries, does not have the same privileges as the others, and so it wasn't shocking when even the government of the country became a bully when I was trying to change my status. When I turned eighteen, I applied for a work permit, which I got, but after one year, when time came to renew that permit, I wasn't allowed to and was asked to find ways to return to Haiti. I felt like after thirteen years, with all my foundation and education being done in the country, I would be able to legally become a citizen, but one after the other, I got declined and blocked, and no one was able to help me. At some point in time, I felt like my Haitian passport would not be able to get me anywhere and that I could stop dreaming big, but oh, how I love that God's plans are always better than ours.

I again reminded myself that when someone accepts Christ into their life and becomes a Christian, it does not automatically solve all their problems, and it will probably be one of the hardest paths they've ever taken. There is no servant of the Lord who has not gone through trials and tribulations, but the difference is that God is there through the pain and everything else. Daring to be different is a bold step, and so it comes with its challenges, but the reward is far greater than what we could ask or think.

For instance, if I am angry or someone has hurt me, it affects everything else that I do for the time that I am mad or sad. It is very difficult for me to hide my expressions and my moods are most times reflected on my face and in my behavior. So, I would rather deal with an issue head-on than have it prolonged because it affects how I move or my day. I find myself in my thoughts and I keep going over incidents that might have been and those that have happened, but I always remind myself that I too have gotten people angry about some things, especially God. Yet, still He does not stay mad at me. To me, having God does not mean that I won't sin, but unlike the people in the world, I am at a greater advantage because I do have God, and if I repent and confess sincerely, I know I am straight with Him.

> Matthew 11:28 - 30 says, *"Come to me, all you who are weary and burdened, and I will give you rest. Take my yoke upon you and learn from me, for I am gentle and humble in heart, and you will find rest for your souls. For my yoke is easy and my burden is light."*

God is indeed the best source of strength that we have. When something is wrong, our first instinct is to look for someone to run to for help; or, if you're like me, it is to shut down and close off. It is so hard today to find someone who will stick by you through thick and thin so your best bet at the end of the day is God. I have tried therapy and sadly, I met some pretty bad therapists, like I mentioned earlier, instead of helping me, they were taking what I was saying and telling it to people. I eventually met a therapist who would hear me out, and who became exactly what I needed for the season I was in. My mother always reminded me that some things that were going on in my life, people just didn't have to know. "Let it be between you and God," she would say. He keeps the darkest of secrets safe! I often brag about my best friend because I feel like she was created for me, and she meets me halfway, but sometimes, I don't tell her some things. When you make your full self-available to everyone, you are at a higher chance of being placed under the microscope to be examined.

What I have also learned so far is that you should constantly remind yourself how important you are because the value you place on yourself will determine how you live, how you see yourself, and how you react to things. See yourself as God sees you!

Ever since I started my blog, *Life in Writing* (LIW), criticism was something that I was open to. While some appreciated and applauded me for being real, open, and honest, others would try to bring me down for that same thing. Someone went as far as judging me for speaking about God all the time in my blogs or for not speaking about things they think I should speak about.

As a child of God and a believer, I believe it is my responsibility/duty to speak about Him. I have experienced Him personally, and have seen His goodness in my life. I strive for perfection, but I am mindful that I am an imperfect human being, and so, my relationship with Him is also not perfect, which is seen at times. I've explained some of the moments where I got mad at God and questioned His Word, but He has never stopped loving me, keeping me, protecting me, and blessing me throughout my imperfections.

That's why I center my blogs around God, no matter the topic. It is rather fitting that I consult Him, find the application in His Word, and share it. God has a purpose in everything, so I must find and understand the purpose. I must seek Him to know what His plan is for me and how I can fulfill His will. My goal as a Christian is to be the salt of the Earth, bringing people to Him. As I always say, while my blog serves many purposes, its main objective is to be used as a tool for ministry. Recently, I was challenged in an area of weakness in my life, and I had to be on my knees every night seeking God for strength. I came across the song, "All I Want," by James Fortune, that I used to feed my spirit. It says, *"Jesus it's you, who understands the language of my tears, the broken parts of me that haven't been healed, cause you're working on me and you're still working on me. Jesus, it's you! And all I want is more, more of you!"*

[4]Every time I listened, I cried because I knew what these words meant to me as an individual, especially when my own emotions tried to convince me that I'd never be good enough like one of the verses said.

It is difficult to maintain a walk that comes with challenges and temptations, but knowing who you are, and whose you are, propels you to continue to persevere on the walk because you know your *alignment*. Your *spiritual alignment*! Alignment to me is when things line up together harmoniously, and spiritual alignment is not just a state of being in line with God, but when your whole being is in tune with everything that concerns godliness.

This path is compared to hiking, when you encounter boulders/rocks in the way, and fallen trees/branches. You might get knocked over by one or miss a fall, but you don't stay down. I have tried staying down many times where

I've fallen, and God is always there, telling me to get up *My child. Up! Up!* And He keeps reminding me of my purpose.

I am just twenty years old, and don't have it all figured out, but I believe no matter how old one gets, you will never have it all figured out, but along the way you learn and grow. No matter what is thrown at you in life, you've got to overcome it. Personally, the only one who has succeeded in helping me do that is God.

That's why I will continue to speak about Him whenever possible, because He knows best and I've experienced His unfailing love over and over. Someone once said the scariest verse in the Bible is Matthew 7:21, when Jesus was speaking to a crowd of people, and said, *"Not everyone who says to me, 'Lord, Lord,' will enter the kingdom of heaven, but only the one who does the will of my father who is in heaven."*

Honestly, I think that's a scary verse, and the person who asked me the question, "Why do I speak about God so much?" may have actually meant something like this, but in the end, the question that should be asked and answered is "What is the Father's will?" As long as you know the answer and you are fulfilling it wholeheartedly, then it should not be that scary. If I know who I am, *whose* I am, my purpose, and I understand my alignment, I will continue to speak of Him.

There is one thing I always remember about people who bully and cause pain: they are going through something, and sometimes they see something in you that they wish was in them, or something that scares them. I can be very gullible at times, and it took me a while to learn how to be a "dasheen leaf," like my sister would say, which means, being able to let things slide off my back to the point where they don't bother me anymore. In everything that you do, you will get people who will like you for it and dislike you for it, but I had to understand that at the end of the day, there is only one man I had to answer to, and that is God. If what you are doing or believe in is pleasing in His eyes and aligns with His Word, then do it and stand up for it. Too many times, we run away from our calling because we fear judgment, lack of support, and naysayers. That was me a few years back, until I realized that life would be boring without these kinds of people, because if everyone agreed with you and was okay with everything that you did, then it'd all be fake. Never let the odds keep you from doing what you know in your heart you were meant to do; the struggle is part of the story.

There is more to life than our problems and our sins; there is more than our troubles and pains. There is so much more that life has to offer, if only we would open our eyes and our hearts to see it, grab it, and accept it. Let every trial be a lesson and a teaching moment, so when something similar comes your way, you can deal with it better than the last time. And above all, let your past be your past!

Steve Maraboli once said, *"The truth is unless you let go, unless you forgive yourself, unless you forgive the situation, unless you realize that the situation is over, you cannot move forward."*[5] We are all humans, and we were born sinners, so if there is one thing we're going to do, it is making mistakes. If God can forgive and erase these mistakes, then why do we as humans hold grudges and dark clouds over ourselves and others?

My favorite set of verses in the Bible is Psalms 103:1-5:

> *Praise the LORD, O my soul; all my inmost being, praise his holy name. Praise the LORD, O my soul, and forget not all his benefits—who forgives all your sins and heals all your diseases, who redeems your life from the pit and crowns you with love and compassion, who satisfies your desires with good things so that your youth is renewed like the eagle's.*

The reason why I like these verses so much is that the Hebrew word for *all* is *pas,* and it means *without limitation.* The verse says, "...and not forget *all* His benefits – who forgives *all* our sins and heals *all* our diseases." God does not only focus on part of us, but He has also completely redeemed us from our past, our mistakes, and everything. A clean, white slate! The greatest act of love that we as humans have ever received is the cross. Jesus died on cavalry for us to become new, and to be able to live life more abundantly. Being in Christ gives us hope, assurance, and we gain freedom through His precious blood, and it's all thanks to grace.

I don't think thankful is the word that I can use to describe my life right now. I am indeed thankful, but it is so much more than that. I've come a long way, and I made this quote that I now say, "A present without a past is unheard of!" I love my story and my past because it made me into who I am today, and whenever I get the time, I thank God every day for writing my story as He did. If you had told me a few years back that the things I find myself doing and being a part of now would happen, I would tell you that you were lying. My writing took a turn for the better; I no longer indulge in dark poetry, self-pity, or sing the same tune all the time, always asking, "God, why me?" Instead, I write pieces that bring hope and encouragement to people. I successfully turned my blog into a business, and continue to share my story, providing advice and positive light on issues that affect teenagers and young adults like me. I am one step closer to making my dream a reality by establishing a nonprofit organization called the Michel Hands and Hearts organization, which assists immigrants in finding the strength to go on and fight, because I know and remember what it's like to be a foreigner in a country. I've never been prouder to be a Haitian than I am right now because I've come to understand and know that it doesn't make me who I am or define me. While trying to be my true self, I've learned to stand for my background, and my nationality has played a vital role in my story, and for that I am grateful.

God keeps using me and making a path for me, and though I may not have the right words to express how I feel, I know that He is continuing to bless me beyond my understanding, and what I need.

One of my biggest testimonies now is that I made it to the United States, studying journalism at the Florida Memorial University. Why is it a testimony, you might ask? It is because I saw God move everything that was in my way of getting to where He wanted me to be, one-by-one. The same Haitian passport that I wanted to get rid of and that I believed would not get me anywhere, God made what seemed like the impossible, possible. My journey to the United States was not easy, but God's timing is always perfect! He worked everything out and provided the funds. He was there with me at immigration, at the embassy for my visa, and everything. I will never stop boasting about God because He is real and always present. I am happy to say that I am not lucky, but blessed. His Grace and love are sufficient. I have also reunited with my birth mother after eleven years, and while it is taking some time to adjust because we are so different, I love the fact that God is in this. The natural bond between us continues to grow and flourish, and I am amazed every day as to how far we get day-by-day.

I am thankful for family and friends who continue to support me and pour into my life daily. My mother continues to be my pillar and the one I lean on the most. She is the definition of a praying woman, and one who finds favor with God. As soon as something goes wrong in my life and I let her know, her first statement, before providing me with any advice is, "Let's pray about it!" She continues to share her prayer time with me, devotions, and invests in everything that I do. But, in the end, all the glory and honor belong to God, for His unmerited love and His amazing grace.

Before I minister my poems anywhere, I always sing the lines from the Casting Crowns' song "Nobody," which says, *"I'm just a nobody trying to tell everybody, all about Somebody who saved my soul. Ever since He rescued me, He gave my heart a song to sing, I'm living for the world to see nobody but Jesus. I'm living for the world to see nobody but Jesus."* [6]

At the end of the day, that is the only thing that I wish to do, and I believe that no matter how many times I fall, I will rise above every situation because of that little something called grace, which I don't deserve but it was gifted to me by the one who created me and loves me most in this world.

Based on a quote I saw on Pinterest which was said to have been written by Susanna Wesley, "I am content to fill a little space if God be glorified!"

My tip for others is to always remember that there is no one like you on earth. There is only one of you! No one goes through the same things as you; it might be similar, but it is never the same and to always be kind to others. It took one girl who was kind enough to speak to me and be my first friend in an unfamiliar place to open a pathway to others.

God created you uniquely, a masterpiece after His image!

My encouragement to you who have read my story is to walk in your purpose; put God first and He'll do the rest!

Again, there's more to life than the problems we face, the pain we feel, and the burdens we bear.

It started with a little Haitian girl, confused, and lost, to a Haitian woman, with a vision and on a mission!

There's more!

Love,
Serge

Poetry/ Spoken Word Collection II

Go On

Hold on a little while longer.
Search a little deeper.
Read a little further.
Strive to be bolder.
Walk a little braver.

You will reach.
You will find.
Just grind.
I beseech.

Don't lose hope.
Cope.
Don't fear.
Bear.
Don't standstill.
Fulfill.

While it may be hard
Don't let down your guard.
Remember who you are.

For you are rare.
Know that someone cares
Out there, somewhere!

The finish line may seem far.
But don't give up just yet.
Please don't fret.
Because, just like a star,
there's a source of strength
From whom you can replenish
Your weary soul.
Then you'd be able to finish
The race of life at great lengths.

Hold on a little while longer.
Search a little deeper.
Read a little further.
Strive to be bolder.
Walk a little braver.

And find the courage
To go on.

CAN I MEASURE YOUR WORTH?

Can I measure your worth with a number on a scale?
Can I rate you from one to ten?
Can the color of your skin define who you are or who
you'll become?
Can the last name you carry dictate how far
you'll reach?

Society has tried to create an idea as to who should be
and shouldn't be.
Who deserves and who doesn't?
Who lives and who dies?
The idea of supremacy, war against humanity.
A battle of religion instead of seeing the real true God.
Should I put a sign to your character as a person?
Should your future be known by the lines on
your hands?
Should your vaccination status be the key to your
access in the world?
Should letters be placed on your identity?

The more silent we become, the more we scream
acceptance.
We dim our light and our voice in this troubled world,
When we should be the loudest!
So, before it is too late, let's take a stand.
Be the Voice; be the light!
For eternity stands above all.

Can I measure your worth?
The answer will always be no!

AMAZING GRACE

It's like the wind.
You feel it, but you can't see it!
Undeniably magical!
A strong presence,
Without a beginning or an end.

There's More

It's unlike any other.
Struck by greatness,
Unmatched by human likeness!
I stand in awe of such wonder!
It's like the wind.
You feel it, but you can't see it!

It's like warmth and kindness.
Love and goodness.
A perfect ensemble.
In tune and harmonious.
Dignified and righteous.
It's like the wind.
You feel it, but you can't see it!

It brings life to the lifeless.
Unbreak the broken.
Freeing chains, bound by selfishness.
Recovering what may have been forgotten.
Bringing in the joy of rebirth.
Erasing past and present wrongs.
It's like the wind.
You can't see it, but you know it's been there.

Just like the trees dance to the wind's rhythm.
The leaves fall in worship.
So is the grace that is bestowed.
Living inside.
Forming and continuing,
A work that has just begun.
It's like the wind; you can't see it

But you know it's been there!
It leaves a light that shines so bright.
Bright enough that the world can see,
That I am no longer who I used to be!
So, I bask in that Light.
I walk in the path that has been made clear.
With every step ordered,
I am becoming what I was meant to be.
The child of a king
Royalty!

So, it's like the wind.
You feel it, but you can't see it!
You can't see it,
But you know it's been there!

Amazing grace that saved,
Saved a wretch like me!

HOPE

The Hope we hold is so bold and grand
That even the devil can›t withstand.
He'll try his best to bring us down
And try to make Jesus frown.
For there›s a power in hope that Satan doesn›t
understand.

IT TAKES ONE MAN

It took the Son of God, Jesus Christ, to give us life in
this world of sin!
It took one black woman, Rosa Parks, who initiated the
civil rights movement, defying segregation laws!
It took one man's "I can't breathe" to reopen the
eyes of many!
Eyes that have been shut to the sting of system-
atic racism.
To hear voices that have been silent on the issue of
oppression,
To see action and yet again a movement uprising.

It takes one man!
Only one!

But, while You're here waiting and praying,
For someone else to take a stand,
To speak for you when you have a voice.
To pave your way when you have those same rights,
Is dumbfounded!
Never! Never have I ever been so struck
To see men and women hurt.
While others spew nonsense when their arguments are
unfounded,
Their criticism? Unwarranted!

So, while you sit and wait,
Hope and hope again.
That someone or something will create the change,

Why don't you be the change you want to see?
Doesn't have to be big, nor small,
For it takes one man! Only one!
One small act of kindness, one compliment.
A helping hand and a kindred heart.
It takes one man, only one
To make the difference we so desperately need!

BE YOU TI - FUL

I feel like every time I look in the mirror,
instead of loving what I see,
instead of thinking good thoughts,
I see every label that has been placed on me.
Every adjective they used to describe who I am per-
ceived to be.

I fail over and over to see the reflection that I see.
I hear the voices of the people who have called me
ugly, fat, and unworthy of love.
Maybe you as well have heard the same or worse,
that you're too skinny, thick, black,
and the list goes on.

Every time these words are spoken, they create a hole,
that gets deeper as time goes by,
leaves you to wonder if you'd ever be beautiful,
if you'd ever be enough to fit in.

Yet, I find myself back in that mirror.
And every time I see the reflection,

The words rush back to me.
I see them printed, bold and clear.
Pointed at me, staring and waiting,
for me to accept and believe.

Then, the war begins.
Every time I try to not think of these things
They overpower every single good thought that was
left in me.
Words that cause pain still form part of me.
It reached a point where I couldn't bear.
So, I did what I thought was best.
I began to judge myself.
I gave in and accepted,
And finally admitted,
I do not like what I see!

I lost sight of God's Word,
where He says that I am made in His image
and likeness,
His perfect masterpiece.
Then, He whispered in my ears,
"Oh no, My child, you are to me what you are
meant to be."
You see, people's opinions and perceptions have a way
of trampling over
Our self-confidence and the little bit of self-love we
have left.

In the end, we lose every ounce of gratitude and
appreciation

for the one who deserves it,
and that's us.
The next time I looked in the mirror
I saw what God sees.
I started to speak to myself, saying,
"Hey, you! You are beautiful; you are whole, marvelous, a
perfect masterpiece,
you are the clay that was sculpted by the best potter."

Let's step out and claim our beauty.
Step out and claim our identity.
For we are just who we're meant to be.
Be youti - ful!

WITH CONSENT

It's mine! Rather, it's His temple,
tread carefully! I advise!

You don't touch; you don't fantasize.
You don't speak of, nor do you describe.

It's not a car, so there is no test driving it!
Don't even ask because I've reached my limit!

I'm not a hypocrite, nor perfect, so I'm gonna be real
I'd rather you hear the truth than my fake appeal.

Yes, I did; I've failed on my promise once,
but the good thing is that God gave me another chance.

There's More

So, I'm taking the high road; no more bending.
Can't you see how amazing is the gift of repenting?

You don't feel, You don't look,
You don't pretend, because that chapter of sin has been
closed in this book.

Not sure if you know how hard it is breaking soul ties,
so I'd rather stay alone than compromise.

Coming through with an ultimatum?

I'm guessing you don't understand the spiritual warfare;
hence, why you're being so dumb.

I'd rather you keep asking and be rejected,
than to force yourself on me and be tormented.

It was just you and me, when it should've been Him,
you, and I,
so I did us both a favor by removing you out of the equa-
tion, and here's my reason why:

I'd rather it just be me and Him equally,
than to be yoked with you unequally.

I've come to realize that it's not an easy road,
but letting you go was the first step, and my
heaviest load.

Temptations will come as many as can be,

but I know that, with God by my side, I'll win this fight,
and wait for the one who was meant for me.

IF DEATH HAD A VOICE

I don't think we ever understand the gravity of it,
The sting that it brings,
and the pain that it leaves.
When every single memory flashes before our eyes,
within seconds, and leaves us feeling numb.

Makes us wonder if it had a voice,
where it would speak and give us the time, the date,
the hour, the second, and the minute.
So, that maybe, just maybe, we'd prepare ourselves
for the moment the ones we love so dear would leave
us behind.

It would remind us of the time we have left,
where moments shared become more meaningful,
where every second is cherished,
and we're reminded that memories are timeless trea-
sures of the heart.

Makes us wonder if it would speak of the good times,
and remind us that the good outweighs the bad.
To give more flowers and compliments,
savoring every moment and each other's company, while
there's still time.

It would remind us of the three words worth
sharing each day,
where it's not taken lightly, but is rather held on
a pedestal,
where each utterance is most profound.
I love you! To infinity and beyond!

If only death had a voice,
Maybe, just maybe, it would be bearable,
it would give us warnings and signs,
so that we'd be able to endure when it has come.
Then, we'd not be sad, feel empty, and live in regret,
but rather, happy knowing we made use of the
days granted,
with the ones we love so dear.

If it could speak, we only hope,
it would remind us of eternity and the promise of the
afterlife.
Where we look forward to seeing the smiles
we›ve missed,
and the hugs we›ve practiced in our dreams.
Oh, the difference it would make,
If death had a voice!

THERE'S MORE

I think it›s in our nature to only see what›s in front of us,
and that often leads us to lose sight of what could be.
We place ourselves in a box
Where we don't venture outside of our comfort zones,

Where what seems unfamiliar becomes dangerous.

Caged by our thoughts and ideas,
Indecisive of what should and shouldn't be,
Blocking the blessings that are meant to be
By closing off to a world full of possibilities.

I think it's time we open our eyes,
See a little clearer,
Create a bigger picture.
I think it's time to open up the box and show ourselves,
Letting in the light, to shine a little brighter.

It takes one man to create change,
So let's take the first step and claim our domain.
It is time to stop,
Hiding all our talents, saying we've got none.
When we haven't given ourselves the opportunity for our
imagination to run free.

There›s more to what we feel,
More to what we see.
More to everything that is to be!

Let's rise to the test,
And don't give up yet,
Rising to the challenge
To be the best that we can be,
For there's more than we can see!

Additional Poems/ Spoken Word

BE IT LOVE OR FRIENDSHIP

If flowers don't suffice

Let my words be enough.

While everything else may seem apart

May our connection last.

While we stride into the unknown

Reminiscing on memories

and flashbacks that we had

let it be known that this was true.

The laughter, the smiles, the ups and downs,

the pains and trials we try to forget but,

That›s when we realized these things made us
what we are.

There is no love without hurdles,

no friendship without hardships,

no commitment without trust.

There are times when we question loyalty,

question the what-ifs and the whatnots,

and the countless misfortunes that we›re scared of.

These moments served as a reminder that all we
needed was the love we gave, and all we'll ever need is
that love.

Oftentimes, we dream of glamour and finer things,
but I'm so glad we never lose sight of what we have or
hope to be.

The moments we wish to forget what we want and
remember what we deserve,

what is worth fighting for and how many fights we have
left within,

To muster up the courage to face this head-on.

I'm here for you and you for me,

Hand-in-hand and side-by-side.

Be it love or friendship,

Let this be what it's meant to be!

RUNAWAY

I wish I could runaway
To a place filled with peace.
A place where love reigned supreme
A place where it's just you and me!

I wish I could runaway
To a world so very far away.
Where the birds always sing
And the grass is always green.
Where the air is always fresh
And money isn't a thing!

I wish I could runaway
To a time where I'd hurt no more.
To a time where there's no pain, no famine, no grief.
Where war isn't a business,
Where illness is a myth!

I wish I could runaway
To your arms right now as I write.

Cause when I'm there, I'm safe, I'm alright.
Cause you're my peace, my happiness, my breath of
fresh air, my reason for loving, my reason to care.
My light at the end of the tunnel,
My strength when I fight
So I wish I could run away,

Run away, with you tonight!

THAT GIRL IS GONE

Oh man, I'm tired!

I've had enough!

You see, over and over, I say these words, yet I find
myself back at it again!

It's a pattern,

like a song on repeat!

That toxic energy and vibe you bring,

Keep calling me in!

Oh man, I tried!

Tried to pull back!

Made a complete turn only to find me here,

Back to you!

Back to what gives the thrill!

Like a drug that has me hooked,

Hooked on a feeling,

an adrenaline boost!

Until slowly, but surely, it starts to take effect,

It begins to hurt, yet I keep wanting more.

Until it starts to destroy,

Destroy not only my inside, but the outside,

My character and who I used to be.

You took my identity!

Oh man, I quit!

Enough is enough!

It may be too late because the damage has already
been done,

But there is only so much one can take!

There's More

As of now! I mean NOW,

That GIRL is GONE!

The girl who sat and took it all in

Silenced herself, hid behind her tears,

And walked on shells!

SIR! Mr.! Haven't you had enough?

You keep taking and taking from me,

Walking and walking over me,

Belittling and reducing me to what suits you!

Though my scars may not be physical, and we create the
perfect picture,

It's about time I call it In.

Round it up and face it,

You have NO power over me!

Instead, you're a weak man,

Looking for something to give your distasteful
life meaning.

But that something and someone is not me or any other.

The realization may be late, but

SIR! Mr.!

Oh man, I'm DONE!

That GIRL is GONE!

MOMMA, YOU'RE GOD'S BLESSING

If I were to write about the many reasons why
I should celebrate you every day,
and not only every second Sunday in May.

Papers would be no more, ink nonexistent,
for there is so much to say.
I am so glad that the word *Abortion*,

Never existed in your vocabulary, even if you were
only sixteen,
and your parents kicked you out, and you had to be
on your own.
Then I'd ask you, what about the pain endured by those
who can never have a baby?
Leading them to believe that God's love is at
best a maybe!
Or you were happily married to Dad, and you saw me as
an additional blessing to this union.
Or maybe, just maybe, you saved my life and took me,

not flesh of your flesh, but miraculously your own!

A gift that would change your life forever.
The circumstances under which you became Momma
don't matter much,
because you are God›s blessing to me!

All the professions, placed in one, I find in you!
The counselor, when I cried for the petty things and
overreacted for nothing.

The police officer who arrested me and kept me from going to the places I thought were best, and doing the things that sometimes you won't even address!

The doctor for every little pain that I felt, and most times, it was nothing.

The fashion police who would send me to change my clothes a million times, until I looked somewhat close to perfection!

In times of hurt, your words captivated my heart, working what some called mummy magic!

But, I see now that it was grace and love, as you helped me through time so tragic!

I thought you were nosy when you kept going through my room, going through my phone, asking all the questions that would send me mad, and wanting to be an adult, just to get a place of my own!

Always wanting to know, who's the guy I was hugging? Where and whom I was going places with?

All these things made me feel like you didn't love me, or were just the hot flashes kicking me.

Had me guessing, if it was menopause? Or just you, being a mom!

Later down I realized that you didn't only love me, but you also didn't want me to repeat your mistakes!

Wishing better for me every day,

praying to God and asking Him to bless me in every way!

Momma, I know words aren't enough, actions can only do much

But may I say that because of all this nagging and fussing and sometimes, even making you second guess your choice of having me, you've loved me unconditionally.

I don't think my first salary would be enough

To repay you for so much

Nine months, maybe less, maybe more

Eighteen years! Maybe more, you've taught me what is meant to be a mother, and maybe one day, if God were to bless me with children of my own, I'd rather do it the way you raised me!

It may not seem like I appreciate it all or show you that I care as much I just want you to know that you are loved, honored, cherished and most of all protected, but if there's one thing I know without a doubt, Momma, you're God's blessing to me!

A WORLD OF PAIN

What is there to gain?
In a world of pain.
Is there anything to learn?
One of my concerns.

A world where justice is not served,
Where peace becomes something that we don't deserve.
Troubles left and right, that gets on our last nerve.
Yet, we destroy so much, we can't conserve.

What is it in this world of pain?

Where hatred is the new way of love?
Where no one can strive to be above?

Where division says unity?
Where we sleep with one eye open for there is calamity?

What is it in this world of pain?

Murder, the new game,
Sadness, the refrain

Silence, the laughter
Starvation, the new chapter.

What is it in this world of pain?

Leaders, politicians, kings, and queens!
We shout your name, a change please!

What would it take?
To amend this mistake.

What is it in this world of pain?

That we perish,
When instead we should cherish,
The moments of freedom and good we have established.
Let us put our heads together and accomplish
Something that can make a difference and replenish.

What would it take in this world of pain?

ENDNOTES

1   Maya Angelou, Letter to my daughter (Random House Publishing, 2008).

2   Rick Bezet, Be Real Because Fake is Exhausting (Ada: Baker Publishing Group, 2014).

3   Bezet, Be Real Because Fake is Exhausting.

4   James Fortune and Ayron Lewis, "All I Want," FIYA Music/ Entertainment One, track on Dream Again, 2019, YouTube.

5   Steve Maraboli, Unapologetically You: Reflections on Life and the Human Experience, Book III (Port Washington, New York: A Better Today Publishing, 2013).

6   Casting Crowns, Mark Hall, Matthew West, Bernie Herms Label, "Nobody," Provident Label Group LLC, a division of Sony Music Entertainment, track on Only Jesus, 2019, YouTube.

Lightning Source UK Ltd.
Milton Keynes UK
UKHW051551181122
412328UK00025B/86